D0578307

THE WAYS OF FLOWERS

Victoria

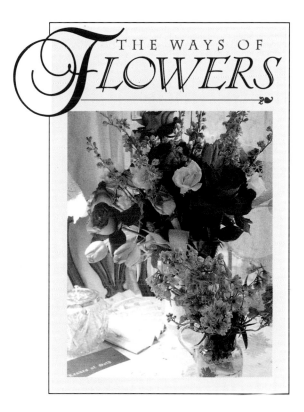

THE WAYS OF FLOWERS

Text by Tovah Martin

HEARST BOOKS

New York

Copyright © 1994 THE HEARST CORPORATION

All rights reserved. No part of this book may be reproduced or utilized in any form or by any means, electronic or mechanical, including photocopying, recording, or by any information storage and retrieval system, without permission in writing from the Publisher. Inquiries should be addressed to Permissions Department, William Morrow and Company, Inc., 1350 Avenue of the Americas, New York, N.Y. 10019.

Recognizing the importance of preserving what has been written, it is the policy of William Morrow and Company, Inc., and its imprints and affiliates to have the books it publishes printed on acid-free paper, and we exert our best efforts to that end.

Library of Congress Cataloging-in-Publication Data

Victoria The Ways of Flowers—1st edition
      p. cm.
  ISBN 0-688-12591-3
  1. Flowers. 2. Symbolism of flowers.
GT5160.V53 1994
398´.368213—dc20   94-7913
                                              CIP

Printed in Italy

First Edition

1 2 3 4 5 6 7 8 9 10

For Victoria—
Nancy Lindemeyer, Editor-in-Chief
Bryan E. McCay, Art Director
John Mack Carter, Director, Magazine Development

Edited by Laurie Orseck
Designed by Nina Ovryn

Produced by Smallwood & Stewart, Inc., New York City

Notice: Every effort has been made to locate the copyright owners of the material used in this book. Please let us know if an error has been made, and we will make any neccessary changes in subsequent printings.

Contents

Chapter Four

AT HOME: IN TOUCH WITH THE SEASONS
82

Chapter Five

TENDER CARE: WORKING WITH FLOWERS
102

GALLERY OF FLOWERS
131

Foreword

"Could not resist the French violets, I simply had to have them," wrote a young teacher in diary on her grand tour of Europe at the end of the twenties. And isn't that the way we all feel about the flowers we love? They are truly the jewels we can all afford. When we pin a flower to label, or crown a flower girl in a ringlet of tiny roses, we are the inheritors of a legacy, a ransom as rich as any monarch.

In our homes, flowers make all the difference. A pretty room becomes beautiful with even one well-placed bouquet. For a festive occasion, flowers create a domain for a bride, a graduate, or an anniversary couple.

L.M. Montgomery, the author of "Anne of Green Gables," had very definite ideas about the display of flowers. Never a bouquet, said she, flowers were to be arranged one kind to a vase. All of us have such preferences that make the ways of flowers our very own. In this book, you'll find many, many inspirations to pick from. As for my personal tastes, with apologies to Mrs. Montgomery, whom I have always adored, I will gather from the garden as many flowers as I can hold to make a grand arrangement the way nature has given them to us—all the colors, all the sizes, all the glories. I hope with "The Ways of Flowers," you become very particular about what pleases you. After all, that is the most important thing.

Nancy Lindemeyer
Editor-in-Chief, *Victoria* Magazine

10

THE
SENTIMENT OF FLOWERS;
OR,
LANGUAGE OF FLORA.

BY ROBERT TYAS, B.A., F.R.B.S.,
QUEENS' COLLEGE, CAMBRIDGE;
AUTHOR OF "FAVOURITE FIELD FLOWERS," "FLOWERS FROM THE
HOLY LAND," "FLOWERS AND HERALDRY," ETC. ETC.

In Flowers heath their will to Nature,
And they tell us of a garland that their love endures,
Each blossom symbolises to their garden bowers;
On its bosom a sweet hostage bears.

WITH SIX COLOURED PLATES.

Eleventh Thousand.

I remember, I remember,

The roses, red and white,

The vi'lets, and the lily-cups,

Those flowers made of light!

Thomas Hood
I Remember

Braided into necklaces or woven into garlands, flowers have combined colors, moods, and personalities since antiquity. Here, dusty miller, boxwood, and lavender are entangled with demure roses and hydrangea petals. ❧ ❧ ❧

With an almost magical power, flowers weave a tapestry through our lives. They overwhelm the present, they evoke the past, they take us on sentimental journeys. They heighten good times and offer comfort in sadder ones, punctuating and enhancing every celebration they attend. Somehow, when flowers are present, life goes more smoothly. Every flower holds two messages: one from history and folklore and one from our personal and private memories. Happily, many of their associations are universally shared: We all recognize the same pertness in a primrose and the same cheerful optimism in the petals of a petunia.

If ever there was a blossom that smiles at everyone, its face beaming with pleasant recollections, it is the humble daisy. Perhaps because it is so very unpretentious, it has become linked with our happiest moments of childhood. Daisies are the symbol of innocent times, tokens of confidences shared between closest friends. For centuries, they have been plucked petal by petal to discern whether "he loves me" or "he loves me not." Daisies have been strung into garlands and halos to adorn the tresses of young

The flowers of spring (above) — sweet peas, grape hyacinths, and white rosebuds — are traditionally linked with birth. The iris (opposite) has a more mature demeanor — and a very flirtatious

meaning: In the Victorian language of flowers, an armload meant "I have a message for you. Often, that message, which had to be delivered in person, was a marriage proposal. ❧ ❧ ❧

maidens as a symbol of purity. And they have accompanied the transition from girl-hood to womanhood: At one time, they were woven into a crown to be worn by a young woman while she decided whether to accept the advances of a suitor. During the Middle Ages, a double daisy emblazoning a knight's shield denoted that he had won a lady's heart. Perhaps because these flowers are so uplifting and invincible, there is a Celtic legend that claims daisies were created to comfort those who have lost a child.

There is scarcely a flower or twig that the Greeks and Romans did not embroider with a legend. Even the most modest of herbs was connected with a colorful myth explaining its birth or providing it with a purpose. The harsh-smelling herb artemisia, for example, was named for Artemis, Greek goddess of the moon, who possessed powers to protect the health of mortals. And so artemisia was often slipped into the shoes of travelers before they embarked on a journey to ensure a safe return home. The finely cut foliage might not be beautiful, but artemisia is still associated with safety and good health. To this day, it is woven into wintertime wreaths to grace the home with its benevolent influence.

The idea that flowers were once mortals, changed into blossoms by the gods — to

S ome of the most delicate-
looking flowers are
remarkably hearty, and so
especially well suited as
"anniversary" plants. Blossoms
from a snowball viburnum
planted on the day your
grandparents got married give
the gift of bouquets every
summer (opposite). Outside
Paris, the Camélia Blanc
shop offers tender bridal
rose bushes (above). *ﺰﻮ ﺰﻮ ﺰﻮ*

help them escape unwanted amorous advances, as a consolation for the loss of a loved one, or as a punishment for selfish behavior — is widespread in Western mythology. The narcissus, sometimes known as the daffodil, came into being when Echo, a wood nymph, found herself infatuated with Narcissus, a vain mortal who spent his days admiring his own reflection in still waters. Wearied by her unrequited affection, Echo slowly faded away, leaving only the shadow of her voice as a reminder of her misery. The gods, furious over Narcissus's vanity, changed him into the daffodil, a flower that sinks its toes into the damp banks of lazy streams, nodding its flowers downward, always seeming to be taken with its own splendor in the water. Ever since, daffodils have been associated with egotism.

———— ❧ ————

Similarly, it is said that the willow was once a fisherman who failed to bow when a goddess passed by. For his disrespect, he was instantly transformed into a weeping tree, doomed to spend eternity hanging in shame by riverbanks, casting leaves fruitlessly into the water. As a result, the weeping willow has come to symbolize supreme sorrow and bereavement.

(continued on page 24)

Flowers are all the more eloquent when their hidden meanings are known by both the giver and receiver. For the Victorians, white ranunculus carried the message "I am dazzled by your charms" (opposite). If offered as a greeting to guests, it was offset by spurge, a symbol of hearty welcome (above) ❧ ❧ ❧

LILACS

Of all spring's shrubs, the lilac is one of the most heavily perfumed and perhaps the most poetic. The soft colors, the plump spires swaying in spring breezes, and divine aroma all speak of springtime's precious moments. The lilac enjoys a well-seasoned past: *Syringa vulgaris,* the common variety, came to Vienna from Constantinople in 1563. The shrub was embraced as a seasonal favorite and quickly became part of the garden vernacular. Early settlers brought cuttings to America with them. Thomas Jefferson wrote about planting some purple flowering bushes at Monticello in the spring of 1767. And in 1786, George Washington noted that his lilac buds at Mount Vernon were swollen and poised to unfold. Not only can lilacs flourish into stately shrubs from tiny sprigs, but they

typically live long lives despite the very worst weather. In New England, no matter how harsh the winter, springtime is known as the lilac tide, dense with these exquisite plumes. In decades past, to celebrate the beginning of the season, young ladies were crowned with lilacs, either purple or white, during May Day festivals. If a maiden wore the flowers on any other day, it was whispered that she would never marry.

We associate lilacs with a delicate shade of palest purple, but lilacs now bloom in white, pink, wine, blue, and navy, and florets can be the traditional star shape or puffy double-petaled clusters. Modern lilacs have all the aroma of their ancestors, combined with increased hardiness, disease resistance, and a longer blooming span. Nowadays, the lilac tide lasts much longer than the fleeting first two weeks of May. Lilac trees should be pruned every year (new buds begin forming at the juncture where the old spire withers). If you cut a few sprigs to make an indoor arrangement, crush the woody stems lightly to encourage the branches to drink, sink them deep into cool water overnight, then fill a tall vase with them and breathe in springtime all over again.

The laurel, myrtle, primrose, peony, and hyacinth were all mortal once as well. The rose, Queen of Flowers, was once the beautiful Rhodanthe, who was pursued by so many suitors that she finally took refuge in the temple of the goddess Diana. Pitying the maiden's plight, Diana turned her into the ravishing rose; her suitors became the thorns along her stem.

Because they are ripe with associations and legends, flowers have served throughout history to represent and bless the causes of mankind. Iris was the messenger of myth who traveled the rainbow bringing word of divine decisions from heaven to earth. During the Crusades, Louis VII adopted the flower as the emblem of France, and the humble iris was forevermore known as the flower of Louis, or fleur-de-lis, its three petals signifying faith, wisdom, and valor.

Some six centuries later, Napoleon Bonaparte chose the violet as his standard. When the general was exiled to Elba, his supporters wore violets in their buttonholes to signify their hope that he would return to France in the spring, when violet blossoms filled the countryside again. When the symbolism of the flower was discovered, the wearing of violets was strictly banned in France. But the restriction only strength-

ened the affection of Napoleon's supporters for that modest flower and its heavenly essence, and many brave souls hid a violet beneath their clothing to send forth a phantom scent. From that time onward, the violet became the symbol of faithfulness.

Napoleon's adversaries also turned to flowers. When forced out of her homeland by Napoleon, Queen Louise of Prussia hid with her son, later William I, in the fields, weaving garlands of bachelor's buttons to idle away the long hours until the royal family might reclaim its throne. William adopted the bachelor's button as his standard when he claimed his title, and the flower thus became a symbol of unity.

———— ❧ ————

Blossoms have often been enlisted in matters of the heart. From the Garden of Eden onward, countless flowers have been associated with the twists and turns of romantic affection. At one time, young maidens believed that the face of their own true love would be revealed in the night if they put their shoes outside the door and a daisy under their pillow. They also believed that if a young woman rubbed pansies on her eyes, she would fall hopelessly in love with the first creature that came into sight.

The Victorians recognized the splendor of the elegant calla lily, giving it the meaning of "magnificent beauty" in their floral lexicon. At the turn of the century, a bouquet of expensive callas was the ultimate indulgence, bestowed only by serious admirers. ❧❧❧

Artists have long been influenced by the effortless grace of the rose; much garden architecture, especially wrought-iron garden gates, was inspired by its curving petals (left). Another meaning of the full-blown rose is secrecy; at one time, a rose pinned over the doorway of a meeting was considered a promise of confidentiality. ❧ ❧ ❧

But most often, flowers were simply sent as ambassadors of the heart — coy and timid, fervent and ecstatic. Since the beginning of time, suitors have been pressing flowers into the hands of ladies. Although every flower appears to communicate with an eloquence that the heart recognizes, certain ones seem particularly adept at furthering romantic entreaties. The rose, with its silken petals and blushing shades, stands paramount as a symbol of love. The calla lily, cloaked dramatically in white, is the very essence of sophistication and seductiveness.

Other flowers and herbs have been slipped into lovers' hands to send meaningful messages between two hearts. In Greek mythology, Venus, rising from the sea with a myrtle garland on her brow, selected that herb as her emblem of love; in many cultures, myrtle is an essential element of the wedding bouquet. Lilacs, linden branches, and orange blossoms have long been connected with romance and fecundity. The little purple-petaled, yellow-eyed myosotis became so closely linked with romantic entreaties that it was given the common name forget-me-not to reflect the mission on which it is most often sent. Bleeding hearts, with their chains of dangling cordate flowers, are often used to dramatize the agony of unrequited love.

Some flowers take their meaning from the company they keep. When mountain laurel, associated with ambition, is combined with cascades of wild lathyrus, signifying lasting pleasure, and roses for love, the message is congratulatory (opposite). In eighteenth-century European tales, the foxglove was so often linked with frivolous fairies that the flower became a symbol of insincerity (above). ❧ ❧ ❧

In our memories, a flower's petals never curl, its beauty never wanes, its scent never fades. The fragrance of carnations in a family photograph seems just as vivid as it was the evening of a school dance (above). Collected over the years, graphic floral memories are abiding reminders of the flowers in one family's history (right). ❧ ❧ ❧

Queen Anne's lace and hydrangea buds bring to life a reunion photo (right). Miniature rosebuds, entwined with ivy in a grape-vine heart, recall a special occasion (below). The soft color of a solanum vine will remind a mother of her child's infancy (opposite).

ℰℋ ℰℋ ℰℋ

Although flowers and romance have always traveled arm in arm, it was not until the eighteenth century that an entire "language" of flowers was created. The writer Lady Montagu, the wife of the British ambassador to the Ottoman Empire, observed that Turkish maidens dispatched and received messages "written" in flowers. The communication seemed so very precise, and the device so enticingly flirtatious, that in 1718 she sent an example of floral correspondence to a friend in England. The idea of spelling out messages with flowers quickly caught on. Every flower was assigned a meaning, and the basis for the language flowed directly from the legends of mythology. The first floral dictionary was published in England by Elizabeth Wirt in 1829. Florigraphy, or the language of flowers, so captured the imagination of friends and lovers that every etiquette book in the late nineteenth century included an explanation of how to shape flowers into sentences. Yet every dictionary

affixed a slightly different definition to each blossom, giving the language of flowers a delightful ambiguity and mystery.

Victorians continued to practice the art, despite — or because of — the suspense inherent in the uncertainty of interpretation; only if a person happened to have the same dictionary as the recipient of his bouquet could he be certain his message would be properly translated. By pairing various flowers, complex thoughts could be conveyed. If a nutmeg geranium (signifying an expected meeting) was tucked beside a passionate red rose, a tryst was undoubtedly being proposed. If the same geranium was returned with an anemone (meaning "forsaken") and a snapdragon ("presumption"), the overture was being sternly refused. A ranunculus meant "You are radiant with charms." A jonquil meant "I desire a return of affection."

The precise color of flowers also held different shades of meaning. With roses, coral petals meant admiration, golden petals jealousy, and red petals passion and desire. Even the incline of the bud — whether it faced left or right — had a bearing on the message. A hydrangea turned to the right clearly said, "I am cold," but if the petals were facing left, they meant "You are cold." A flower sent with petals facing downward meant the exact opposite of its upright position; a star-of-Bethlehem, for example, normally conveyed purity, but a downturned sprig meant something entirely different!

——— ❧ ———

Before long, romance was not the only language that flowers were speaking for the Victorians. Any excuse would serve to send a bouquet message. Congratulatory arrangements might be composed of palm leaves for victory, a rose for encouragement, lavender for luck, and some tightly folded buds to signify a promise for the future. Primroses were used to symbolize youth; the laurels that crowned Roman victors still conveyed the heights of glory.

A farewell corsage might contain sweet peas for departure, plum blossoms for fidelity, and forget-me-nots and rosemary for remembrance. Flowers sent to a friend in mourning might have a red poppy for consolation, some red geranium blossoms for comfort, snowdrops for hope, and ivy for friendship.

While we no longer send bouquets with such intricate, hidden messages in the petals, or recall all the tales of ancient mythology, many of the legends and meanings forged so long ago still cling to flowers. Flowers have spoken well through history, and they continue to touch our most tender emotions.

Red sweetheart roses, the flowers of passion, have become a traditional gift for lovers throughout the world. One look at their petals conveys the fire and fervor of romance as no other flower can. ❧❧❧

34

ROSES

The rose has been sacred since antiquity. It was the Greek poet Sappho who first proclaimed it the Queen of Flowers, and as such it was eminently suited to serve as an emblem of Aphrodite, the Greek goddess of love and beauty, as well as

the symbol of Dionysus, the god of revelry. The Romans became so enamored of roses that they scattered them through the streets on feast days, slept on pillows filled with their petals at night, and crowned their heroes and victorious athletes with wreaths made of them. Eventually, roses became symbols of peace and prosperity, and praise as well. Today, certain petal colors bear special meanings. The white rose adorns brides, is given to children for christenings and birthdays, and is presented at funerals to signify loyalty. A dozen crimson roses celebrate a young lady's coming of age and the beauty of maturity. Blushing pink roses, especially diminutive buds or miniature varieties, speak of youth and modesty, while the glowing yellow rose is bestowed on royalty and on those who have reached the pinnacle of success. According to some traditions, yellow roses imply jealousy and thus are to be avoided in bridal bouquets. So often a messenger of romance, a single rose is frequently sent to speak for the heart when words have failed. Roses seem to patch up life's little quarrels and reaffirm the pleasures of marriage at anniversaries. In the rose's soft petals is a silent declaration that may just be the very embodiment of love.

For all their beauty, roses must be handled carefully if they are to endure in a vase. Since freshly cut stems must be plunged into cool water immediately, florists often go to the field with tall water buckets in hand. Thorns and foliage are gingerly snipped off and the stem tip is cut at a slant. Roses should always be cut when still tightly furled but showing a hint of color. After all, a rose's greatest poetry is expressed when the bud swells, the petals expand, the flower gracefully unfolds.

Pressing fresh flowers and snippets of greenery between glass plates is a wistful way to preserve their beauty for a special moment, as if they have been frozen out of season in the clarity of ice (opposite). ❧ ❧ ❧

lowers accent life's special occasions. They add to the gaiety when the mood is joyous; they soften solemn affairs. A well-chosen flower bud at a christening will define the event, pressing it into your memory forever. A nosegay clutched in your hand as you march forward to receive a diploma will give the moment special significance. Flowers are integral to so many traditions. There is always a sheaf of lilies tucked somewhere in an Easter scene, and primroses are invariably present at later spring feasts. Majestic orchid corsages appear on Mother's Day, and blushing young ladies pin modest camellias to their prom gowns. Wheat and sunflowers adorn front porches on Halloween, while an immense bouquet of chrysanthemums often takes a position of prominence on the Thanksgiving table.

But new floral traditions are being forged as well. Birthdays, wedding anniversaries, a trip abroad, a first formal dance — such personal moments shine when blossoms accent the affair. Labor Day picnics, Thanksgiving feasts, Christmas gatherings, and New Year's parties are infused with

delightful perfume and good cheer when flowers are included in the celebration.

A child's very first celebration comes when family and friends gather for the christening. Such a joyous occasion begs to be marked with festive flowers; such a momentous ceremony provides the perfect opportunity to establish floral traditions that will endure throughout the child's life. Christening flowers should be as fragile and modest as the newly born infant. Barely unfurled buds subtly portray the miracle of birth. White is the traditional color for a christening, but tiny flowers of almost any shade can be slipped into small bouquets. Pastel petals lighten a solemn ceremony, adding a whisper of gaiety. To introduce a dash of color, tuck in grape hyacinths or bluebells for little boys and freshly burst apple blossoms or tightly furled blush pink rosebuds for baby girls.

Any diminutive and delicate blossom might set the mood at a christening. Small sedate buds cushion the billowing starched linen of a christening gown, while frilly wildflowers such as Queen Anne's lace echo its intricate handiwork. Garlands of flowers draped over pews and altar symbolize the unbroken chain of family and friends in the baby's life.

White, the color of innocence, is most often associated with christenings. Tiny blossoms and the freshest blooms of spring, such as lily of the valley and mock orange, are fastened to the sash of a newborn's gown (above). To decorate the church pews, lily of the valley, novelty narcissus, and tiny white roses are tied up with exquisite white ribbon (opposite).

Certain flowers have attended christenings throughout the centuries. Newly sprouted spring bulbs, especially lightly perfumed narcissus, reflect the springtime of life. Spritely primroses, "the sweet infants of the year," lend a touch of color and a hint of mischief to the celebration. Bright-faced buttercups, which symbolize childhood and the sense of wonder unique to youth, can be strewn here and there. But the dainty bells of lily of the valley are most often present at christenings and namings, for those delicate sprays always herald happiness. After the ceremony has ended, a carefully pressed christening bouquet, perhaps preserved in the pages of a family Bible, becomes a cherished memento to be bestowed upon the child years later.

On a birthday, a few stems of a single species are somehow more effective than a buxom bouquet brimming with different flowers. Birthday blossoms are all the more eloquent if they reflect the season — a vase overflowing with daffodils, tulips, or irises on the morning of a springtime birthday; daisies, delphiniums, and larkspur in summer; Japanese anemones, dainty-petaled chrysanthemums,

(continued on page 48)

White ranunculus is often sent to little girls on their birthdays (above). According to one enduring tradition, a dozen unfolding roses in blushing pastel shades and wrapped in bows are delivered to a young lady on the occasion of her Sweet Sixteen (left).

The fragrance of sweet peas grows even more intense after dark, making them the perfect corsage flower for an evening celebration. In an antique silver holder filled with water (above), they will last the night. A marvelous medley of roses, tulips, lilies, statice, and yarrow conspires to create the perfect engagement bouquet (left). ❧ ❧ ❧

THE ESSENCE OF

VIOLETS

At one time, violets seemed to be omnipresent. They danced on dates with debutantes, they adorned the necklines of society's matrons, they arrived at the opera primly pinned to every lapel. However, the violet so popular with Victorian florists was vastly different from the pert little posies we might find today on a woodland ramble, and it was miles away from the so-called African violets, to which it bears no kinship whatsoever. Old-fashioned violets had an aroma second to none. Words could not describe it,

other attars could scarcely match it, and once sampled, that sweeter-than-heaven fragrance was never forgotten. Young ladies were instructed to sniff their violet nosegays sparingly, for the intensely sweet scent overwhelmed the senses.

Victorian nosegays were composed of twenty-five or fifty violets wired together and encircled with a fringe of violet foliage. To streamline the chore of bunching, florists bred a double violet called "Parma," each flower of which was composed of many jumbled petals. To the eye, they were not nearly as endearing as the pert single varieties. But, oh, what a deep, seductive aroma rushed from their tufted hearts.

Scarcely heated greenhouses were devoted solely to violet crops, and shops in the cities bustled to keep abreast of the insatiable appetite for the flower. In addition to the traditional violet hue, florists bred blossoms that were tinted white, pink, and blue. They selected giant-size flowers with sturdy, long stems and excellent keeping quality — but they completely overlooked the aroma.

With time, scent was bred out of most violets. Yet for those who search, there are still fragrant violets to be found — not in the woodlands, but in specialty flower shops. Draw the flowers into a cozy bunch using the leaves as a fringe and wrap a wire snugly around the stems — the nosegay will last throughout the day clutched in your hand. If a bud or two begins to nod its head, sprinkle it with a few drops of water — violets drink through their petals. They will soon stand pert and redolent again. 🙢 🙢 🙢

For an evening at the opera, peach-colored roses enhance any outfit (above). On prom night, shy French wood violets are fashioned into a colonial bouquet surrounded by a frill of deep red roses (opposite). ❧ ❧ ❧

and asters in autumn; boughs of evergreens, hellebores, and paperwhites forced on the windowsill for the winter birthday. Let a favorite color or a special scent furnish the theme. To add a note of mystery, choose a different bloom to punctuate each birthday — a colorful bunch of pert primroses, saucy bachelor's buttons, and other quaint little blooms for the very young; majestic lilies, roses, and callas in adulthood.

For so many functions, a floral tradition is already firmly in place. At proms and sweet sixteen parties, the traditional corsage was composed of camellias or gardenias, in a simple arrangement to be worn at the waist; today, orchids are more popular. But the most meaningful blossoms arrive when they are least expected. A modest bunch of newly plucked blooms placed beside a dressing table hours before a prom accents the preparation, cools the nerves, provides support. A little nosegay from parents or siblings waiting on the breakfast table on the morning of a dance recital or concert subtly conveys their pride. A few flowers slipped into a school locker by a best friend quietly express heart-

felt congratulations when a hard-won victory has been secured. Before a classmate steps onto a plane for a year abroad, a single bloom or simple corsage pinned to his or her lapel at the very last moment makes the departure festive and carries with it memories of friends at home. Flowers are forever fitting, always appropriate. And the simplest so often carry the warmest messages.

Any blossom received from the hands of a lover is instantly laden with tender associations. The meekest wayside wildflower suddenly gains stature when it carries affectionate connotations; the simplest bouquet becomes a masterpiece when fumbling fingers painstakingly labor to balance petals and harmonize colors for your benefit alone. Roses, with their blushing shades, velvety petals, and sculptured forms, are most often sent to express deepest emotions. Perhaps their delicacy touches upon love's tenuous balance, perhaps the slow dance of their furled petals captures the subtle nuances of an unfolding relationship. For a million reasons, roses have always accompanied romance.

And yet, love has so many moods. To express the endless facets of affection, let a ribbon-tied clutch of powdery pale lilacs, symbolic of love's initial awakening, or sprays of pristine lilies express the purity of

Many-petaled pure white roses and phlox, tied with ribbons and garnished with spires of wormwood buttons and phlox, add to the excitement of any event (opposite).

Trumpet lilies sound a celebratory note with their copper speckled throats, especially if they rise from drapes and bows of illusive mesh (above).

ॐ ॐ ॐ

your feelings. Or send a bouquet of clean, neatly choreographed callas to symbolize the sheer beauty of devotion. In love's lighter moments, use daisies to convey the simplicity and joy of companionship. When doubts arise, dispatch a nest of tightly bunched sweet violets to show faithfulness. When storms blow through, exchange heather as a token of hope. In courtship, every flower has meaning, and you compose the message.

Nurtured by bunches of black-eyed Susans and Queen Anne's lace, coaxed by ribbon-caught bouquets of sweet peas and daffodils, romance might well mature into marriage. No matter how simple or elaborate a wedding may be, the ceremony must be sprinkled with blooms. Throughout the ages, in every culture, flowers have attended when vows are exchanged; they have always been carried in the trembling hands of brides and pinned above the pounding hearts of grooms. They have garlanded pews and altars; they have been tossed by the bride and showered over the assembled well-wishers for as long as anyone can remember.

A bouquet composed of white roses is meant to capture the fleeting moment. In the Victorian language of flowers, the delicate, dramatic petals of swan white roses symbolize devotion and worthiness.

There is scarcely an occasion for which roses are not appropriate, whether softening a midday affair or slipping into the shadows of evening. Here, a symphony in coral and maize pastels awaits wedding guests. ❧ ❧ ❧

To create an arrangement that will last throughout the ceremony and be remembered long afterward, mingle various blossoms steeped in matrimonial traditions. Eloquent bouquets might be neatly adorned with calla lilies, which symbolize magnificent beauty; sweet peas, emblems of lasting pleasure; peonies, the blossoms of modesty; or tulips, implying the headiness of love. Tropical flowers bring a hint of opulence, complementing the tucks and folds of taffeta and other finery. Let exotic orchids, gardenias, and stephanotis spill in a lively cascade softened by maidenhair ferns and flowing with ribbons. Delicately tinted blossoms cushion the solemnity of the ceremony in their soft shades, adding to the festive air.

———— ✽ ————

Sometimes, just a change of season is reason enough to plan a celebration punctuated by flowers. Spring is a season of details, when nature's smallest intricacies are noticed. It is the perfect time to add snippets of parsley, frilly sprouts of mugwort, lavender shoots, and heart-shaped violet leaves to nosegays, to bring blossoming twigs of forsythia, apples, cherries, and almonds indoors. Collect hawthorne, the symbol of hope, and sit it on the kitchen table. Wear pearly white sprigs of lily of the

A flower girl's wicker basket overflows with long-stemmed pink sweet peas and paperwhites (right). Extravagant sheer bows tie up a summertime spray of roses, sweet cicely, and philadelphus (opposite). ✽ ✽ ✽

valley in a buttonhole. String garlands of forget-me-nots and violets and wind them in your hair; tuck a few magnolia buds in the brim of your hat; leave a May basket on a friend's doorstep.

Just when everyone is knee-deep in June, Midsummer's Eve provides the perfect excuse to celebrate the seduction of the season. Luminous white phlox, night-blooming jasmine, evening primrose, pinwheel jasmine, peonies, and godetia all pick up shades from moonbeams and fill the evening air with aroma. A few exotic water lilies floating in a shallow dish provide a subtle hint that something mischievous may be afoot.

On the Fourth of July, let sunflowers, foxglove, and poppies preside over the watermelon feasts and pie-baking contests. Crown the victors of the three-legged race with garlands of marigolds, geraniums, and nasturtiums. If the mood is more sedate, set stately spires of delphiniums and larkspur just a glimpse away from the croquet green or badminton court — then pin a spray or two in the band of your sun hat. And when the season draws to its last hurrah, celebrate Labor Day with a grand crescendo of late summer roses, phlox, daisies, Queen Anne's lace, and black-eyed Susans.

Autumn has a wardrobe all its own. The

Even in silk, a white rose caught up in a luxurious swath of tulle defines the elegance of this wedding gown (opposite). Roses and white muscari, only slightly muffled in 'Irish Lace' ivy, are woven into a crown for a midsummer's dance (above).

kitchen table sways under a serendipitous array of flowers rushed in before the last frost. Every spare jug and crock on hand is recruited as a vase; every marigold, zinnia, sunflower, and dahlia that would not survive the night is crowded unceremoniously into any pot that will hold water. The rafters are dangling with deeply aromatic wormwood, mugwort, lavender spears, and sheaves of wheat, tied, strung, and left to dry.

———— 🙢 ————

At Thanksgiving, adorn the dining room table with fiery maple leaves, thorny barberry and inkberry, and branches of rose hips. Feature such wildlings as asters, Joe-Pye weed, rudbeckias, and flowering grasses; offset them with the salvias, sedums, boltonias, and heleniums still stubbornly blooming in the border. Wind roving runners of lacy autumn clematis and hop vine everywhere; sit plump pots overflowing with blooming chrysanthemums in each vacant corner. Scatter the table with nuts, acorns, and pinecones; work an abandoned bird's nest into the centerpiece.

Resplendent red roses, lilies glowing by the firelight, ruffled camellias set floating in silver serving bowls, a few majestic calla lilies arching in graceful curves from a tall crystal vase — any flower with panache does justice to the

Autumn's cornucopia of culinary delights is met and enhanced by an equally bountiful floral harvest (above). Opulent bouquets of sunflowers and berries echo the ivy wandering along the mantel, and fiery orange roses and mountain mint blossoms are muffled by purple phlox (opposite). 🙢 🙢 🙢

sparkle and delight of Christmas Eve. Headily aromatic citrus in leafy clusters, pungent branches of rosemary tipped in a shock of blue petals, myrtle twigs lined with a frill of starry white blossoms — such plants with a past capture the ancient traditions surrounding Hanukkah. It is a season rich in exotic scents: Mingle the full-bodied, familiar aroma of fresh mint with frankincense and myrrh; hang cloves beside the mistletoe.

This is a moment of masterpieces. It is a time of indulgences, when such floral extravagances as proteas, alstroemerias, amaryllis, bouvardias, jasmine, and any other exotic blooms that might catch your eye in the florist's shop should be wrapped up carefully, whisked home, and placed on the mantel for all to admire.

Refresh flowers often through the twelve days of Christmas, adding new accents, picking new themes, playing color against color. Then greet the New Year with garlands of white, the color of freshly fallen snow and new beginnings. Deck the halls with white roses, calla lilies, ranunculus, feverfew, freesias, paperwhites, tuberoses, tulips, papery hydrangeas, lilies of the valley, and other pearl-hued blooms, muffled with boughs of greenery. String garlands of ivy — the emblem of friendship — on mantels and spilling over sideboards; sprinkle sprigs of holly, boxwood, and spruce about, tied with ribbons, softened with lace. For the most eloquent gift of the season, slip a simple clutch of flowers into a friend's hand.

A Christmas gift is smothered in white roses and satin bows (right). Crystal matches the majesty of snow-white lilies suffused in baby's breath (far right). White pine, arborvitae, and cones are enlivened by deep red holly berries (opposite).

THE ESSENCE OF
PRIMROSES

*A*primrose is a promise. It is the essence of springtime condensed into

flower form. Although famed for exciting spring fever, these

unassuming flowers were once responsible for inciting a horticultural

revolution as well. It all started with a rather crotchety old Irish

bachelor, William Robinson, who ranted long and loud against formality in

the Victorian garden. He abhorred the straight lines and clean edges so prevalent

in landscapes of the time, convincing gardeners that a natural garden might

have beauty beyond meticulously clipped

allées. To accomplish the transition, he

enlisted primroses. And so the primrose

path was born, a ramble fraught with racy

curves and flowers scattered willy-nilly in

colors combined with reckless daring. The

blossoms sort of sneak up on you and then

disappear into the forest. Bright colors and woodsy leaves are scattered about, and the smells of the nearby woods prevail. A few primrose flowers in a button-hole or a corsage express the same mischievous impertinence. They are the clowns of floristry, so adept at setting everyone at ease. In the home, a few plants seem

springtime incarnate in all its striking hues, sweet perfumes, sheer rambunctiousness, and unpredictability. Some prim-roses hide their clusters of blossoms in deeply textured leaves; others hold a crown of flowers head and shoulders above the rosette of foliage or poke lone blossoms coyly through the greenery. And who knows what gaudy color combinations those headstrong buds will display when they open?

Primroses are wonderfully adaptable to life indoors. They love to be jumbled close together in a shallow pan, a wooden trough, a terra-cotta window box, or any-thing else that might hold soil. They prefer to snuggle in the shade of a wooded garden, but they can bask in the diffuse light from a nearby window. With generous watering, cool temperatures, and a bed of fluffy moss underfoot, they perform with all the vigor and profusion of the meandering primrose path.

The fluttery wings of the Spencer hybrid sweet peas were specifically created for wearing on the lapel. Here, the subtle-hued flowers fit perfectly in an antique lapel vase.

With flowers' delightful way of reflecting their brilliance on anything close by, it is little wonder that we pin them on lapels and interwine them in our hair. Borrowing a blossom's luster to put a blush on our lips or a glow in our cheeks is an ancient ploy. Long before precious metals were being fashioned into trinkets, flowers were strung into necklaces and wound in flowing hair. They were the jewelry of country peasants and the badge of nobility as well, bestowing their charms with equanimity among people of all stations. The custom of affixing flowers to clothing probably began when a clutched nosegay became too cumbersome to carry and so was slipped into a buttonhole or a neckline for safekeeping. Not only did the little contrivance work effectively, but it caught everyone's imagination as well, adding a touch of gentle softness to even the most formal attire. Simple garlands and little bunches of flowers, so much a part of childhood play — daisy chains, dandelion wreaths, Queen Anne's lace halos, and cowslip balls — naturally found their way onto our clothing and into special occasions later in life.

At first, violets such as Viola odorata *and the double* Parma *violets (below) were valued for their intensely sweet aroma. Wearing lilacs was said to bring forth the romantic properties of the flower. The lilac chain was a favorite of Victorian schoolgirls (opposite).* ❧ ❧ ❧

Flowers could also sound a serious note and provide essential services as well. Because some are so fragrant, they were often used in public places to help disguise the odors of civilization. People carried nosegays of sweet violets as they passed through the crowded marketplace, holding them where their scent could be frequently sampled during public meetings. Physicians and nurses brought handfuls of aromatic herbs on their rounds to dispel the fumes of illness and protect them from infection. In church during the sweltering days of summer, parishioners clutched bunches of violets, wallflowers, mignonettes, heliotrope, and all the sweetest flowers they could find to override the aromas of neighbors gathered

so close together. Eventually, for convenience, those little bouquets were pinned on the breast within easy inhaling distance or tied with ribbons around the wrist to leave hands free for other work. Thus were born the first corsages and wristlets.

Gradually, flowers appeared more and more often as a part of women's daily apparel. Nosegays and corsages became more elaborate, combining many different blossoms, enhanced with lace, and offset by a few dainty sprigs of foliage. In addition to the common country flowers that were used at first, cultivated blossoms were presssed into service: Roses, orchids, gardenias, and other exotic flowers added their accents to the silks, satins, taffetas, velvets, and chiffons of party finery.

Gentlemen also wore flowers on their clothing, nonchalantly sporting a simple stem in the brim of a hat or the buttonhole of a coat. Before long, those worn above a man's heart took on special meanings, as tokens of particular beliefs or of fraternity; even political factions enlisted them to carry a message. And while at first any flower would do, in time only a few chosen ones were deemed appropriate to offset a gentleman's wardrobe. Bachelor's buttons (naturally), cinnamon pinks (later upstaged by their cousins, the

The petals of roses, especially the many-petaled centifolia types, stay strong for many hours as hair ornaments, but will last even longer if the stems are soaked the night before in room-temperature water, recut, then wrapped in florist's tape. ❧ ❧ ❧

blossom slipped into a tightly wound bun softens its severity, easing its lines. Sprinkled throughout a confusion of curls, rosebuds or tiny herb blossoms add to the profusion.

By far the most sumptuous and ambitious of all floral headdresses is the halo. Woven of tiny buds, laced with little blossoms, and punctuated by a modest frill of foliage, halos have a magic all their own. The first floral crowns were probably the laurel wreaths placed on the heads of victors and scholars in antiquity. But something so beautiful could not remain a solely masculine adornment for long. Halos took on a puckish persona — after all, fairies and elves reputedly pranced around with petals on their heads. Children have always busied themselves weaving garlands while at play, and can scarcely resist donning their handiwork as crowns. On May Day young virgins would dance gaily, each with a wreath of pure white blossoms in her hair, perhaps with the hope of catching some fine young man's eye. Later, if those flowers had successfully worked their charms, those same maidens were wed with a wreath of flowers on their heads.

Although a full-blown floral garland was a bit extravagant for most affairs, a similar effect could be achieved by tucking a few blossoms into the brim of a hat. In fact, at

A loose garland of yellow roses, hydrangea, dusty miller, nasturtiums, and boxwood is wired onto a frame to be set lightly on the head (left). On a tighter halo of long-stemmed baby's breath, hydrangea, columbine, and carnations, the stems themselves are interwoven to form the base to which flowers are added (above). The crowns are floated in a basin until the moment they are put on.

one time, a hat's primary purpose was to conveniently hold an arrangement of blossoms; it was a canvas of sorts, waiting to be adorned with ribbons, petals, feathers, and any other herald of personal expression.

A flower worn in the hair or on a hat will last only a few hours. A stem soaked in water for several hours beforehand will extend its lifespan, as will keeping it away from the beating sun. Sprinkling the petals of wilted cut flowers with cool water will revive them for a few more hours. If they must endure longer in a corsage or necklace, a few precautions will preserve their grandeur. Florists soak the blooms for several hours in room-temperature water to condition them, then wrap the stems tightly in pliable florist's tape to hold in the moisture. Wires slipped discreetly beneath the florist tape and piercing the calyx precisely position the face of each flower while further stiffening the stem. When wrapped and wired, the blossoms on barrettes, garlands, corsages, and boutonnieres will remain lively for many hours. If an occasion lasts longer, perhaps a small silver or glass lapel vase can be pressed into service. Pinned to a jacket and refilled often, it will keep the flowers strong for days, crisp and colorful as the day they were picked. A corsage or neck garland so precious that it must be kept throughout life can be preserved by pressing a sprig between the pages of a hefty book before the petals begin to wilt. If that book does not become its permanent home, a fetching brooch or locket will keep it close forever.

A halo of fresh hydrangeas (right) or purple solvie (far right) dresses even the simplest hairstyle. White philadelphus and a few leafy sprigs of smilax transform a summer hat (opposite). ❧❧❧

THE ESSENCE OF

SWEET PEAS

Sweet peas have always been serious flowers. Despite their impetuous colors and roving ways, they radiate a rather sober elegance. But the flowers' luscious shades and winged petals are only part of their captivating quality — a heavenly perfume has historically been

their true distinguishing trait. Floating from each fluttery petal is a scent once described as the essence of orange-blossom drenched in honey, then touched by the attar of rose. In 1699 that unforgettable scent lured Father Franciscus Cupani, a Sicilian priest, to invite the first wild sweet peas into his Palermo garden. Those early flowers were com-

posed of a plum upper petal (known as the standard) accented by pale blue wings. Although fancier flowers were being introduced in Europe, he could not resist sharing seeds of his new scented treasure with Dr. Robert Uvedale, a British schoolmaster. Within a few years, maroon and blue sweet peas were popping up all over England. For well over a century, gardeners were preoccupied with all the subtle variations of the bicolored flower. Then, in 1865, 'Scarlet Invincible' came on the scene with its bright ruby-throated petals. Unlike the sparse bicolors, the Invincibles, still available today, brandish their blooms in long, dense sprays and in sparkling hues: fiery reds, icy blues, purples so deep they seem nearly black, pinks so pale they suggest only a hint of frosting at the tips, and marbled, streaked, and bicolored varieties. But the most famous modern sweet pea is the frilly petaled 'Spencer,' which first appeared on the estate of the grandmother of Diana, the

Princess of Wales. Spencers became all the rage with their paper-thin petals carefully arrayed in graceful folds. And yet this new generation of sweet peas, so pleasing to the eye, displayed only a shadow of its incomparable original scent.

Because their petals are so delicate and so transient, sweet peas are rarely pinned to lapels anymore. Today they are primarily coveted as bouquet flowers to be combined with forget-me-nots or lilacs. But they have lost none of their serious sophistication, and their luminous petals still haunt long after the bouquet has faded.

Flowers have always taken on new meanings when brought indoors: Mountain ash was thought to repel witches, linden brought good luck to the household. Yellow Scotch broom displayed indoors conveys humility and neatness. ❧ ❧ ❧

ven if you have acres of gardens at your doorstep, flowers have a place inside your home as well. On dismal days, they are a token of sunnier times; when the garden outdoors sleeps, they are reminders of nature's bounty and beauty. In a bouquet arranged by your own hand, flowers become both more poetic and deeply personal. It was the Victorians who embraced flower arranging with an unsurpassed fervor and elevated the bouquet to an art form that could be enjoyed in every home. At a time when flowers were worshiped as the embodiment of all the gentle graces, blossoms became an essential part of home life. Intimate little arrangements were tucked everywhere to inspire stirrings of the soul and impart the goodness of nature. Every wife and mother could compose an arrangement — eclectic homemade bouquets combining as many different blossoms as they could possibly fit into a vase — to celebrate nature's cornucopia. For formal occasions, many-tiered extravaganzas were concocted, meant to totally dumbfound the assembled guests. Although we no longer preach the gospel of flowers or hope to find salvation in their

Just a few sprigs of delphinium, Queen Anne's lace, and frilly astilbe create an elegant still life (below). Tall spires of bright blue delphinium add color to a pure white room (opposite). ❧❧❧❧

petals, we need blossoms in our homes now more than ever to maintain a closeness with nature and to appreciate the cycle of life.

When flowers first unfold in spring, when the garden shows its first hints of color after the seemingly endless winter, the urge to cut a few sprouts and take them indoors is nearly irresistible. Snowdrops, scillas, grape hyacinths, lilies of the valley, and all of the season's first bulbs are so modest and ground-hugging that they are nearly lost outdoors, especially when patches of snow still blanket the garden, but they turn into

priceless little treasures inside. These tiniest blossoms become prominent when profiled in a row of antique goosenecked apothecary bottles on a window ledge.

Yet capturing springtime is not always easy. In so many parts of the country, the season is a turbulent one, full of fits and starts, days drenched in warm sunshine or torrential rain. Outdoors, the tiny bulbs that emerge often last only a few days before shattering under spring showers. Tulips are especially fragile, hastily dropping petals during the first brisk rainstorm. But their life can be lengthened several days when they are cut in bud, wrapped in newspaper overnight, then nestled close together in a tall vase indoors. And although daffodils are not quite so quickly undone by foul weather, their gentle nuances of color can be lost in the crowd outdoors. In a vase, they seem more precious, capturing the brilliance of sun-warmed days even when the sky is cloudy.

If spring is full of little finds that beg to be admired more closely, summer's profusion seems to seep inside by itself. Bouquets tend to be bountiful and perhaps just a little boastful as well; nothing is quite as proud as a vase bursting with stalks of just one kind of flower. Armloads of daisies, lupines, delphiniums, irises, peonies, roses — all

A double-decker parade of sweet peas, in diminutive vases and glassware, dresses even the plainest kitchen window in spring. The flowers, in all their subtle shadings and winged delicacy, can be found in florists' shops long before the first crocus of the season opens outdoors. ❧❧❧

embody the essence of summer. Such bouquets are bound to linger in your mind's eye, evoking memories of languid, blossom-satiated days long after the season has faded.

———— ❧ ————

Some florists say that all blossoms match one another, that nature never fails in her good taste. Certainly, in the midst of summer, you can try some daring combinations and still emerge triumphant. The secret lies in mixing only two or three shades, and doing so with conviction and in generous quantities. No need to visit a flower shop, even if no garden is at your disposal — the meadows can certainly spare a few stems of black-eyed Susans, Joe-Pye weed, and other prolific wildflowers.

If flowers are to remain radiant for several days, they must be harvested early in the morning when the dew has not yet dried. A bucket of room-temperature water should accompany your foray into the garden or field so the newly cut stems can be plunged in immediately. Although it might be tempting to fill a window with an arrangement set directly on the sill, freshly cut blossoms quickly fade and wilt in a sizzling summer sun intensified through glass. Summer flowers last

(continued on page 93)

Perched drama-tically on a balcony, a classic-shaped urn brims with bright pink 'Flirt' zonal geraniums, all per-forming impressively (opposite). And in a tiny alcove beside a dressing table, shocking red roses in full bloom and streamers of English ivy dangle from a tray of vases in two tiers (above). The stand was a little Victorian contrivance to keep blossoms at eye level. ❧ ❧ ❧

THE ESSENCE OF

PANSIES

Pansies are the garden mischief makers, wearing outlandish color combinations, wandering where they have not been invited but generally welcome wherever they go. They go under many nicknames. In America the species *Viola tricolor* is called Johnny-jump-up, a name that fittingly celebrates the rambunctious ways of what was once a wayside herb. It is also known as bonewort, lady's delight, heartsease, and herb trinity; still another name, love-in-idleness, alludes to the amorous troublemaking for which the pansy has always been famous. The most popular pseudonym, pansy, is derived from the French *pensée*, "to think" or "to contemplate." As Ophelia says in Hamlet, "And there is pansies, that's for thoughts." In Shakespeare's day, pansies were thin-petaled, wispy ramblers with tiny little blossoms. It was not until the nineteenth century that *Viola tricolor* was transformed into the

plump-faced performer we know today. Early in the century, one Lady Mary Bennett made plans for a heart-shaped garden; she sent her gardener around her Surrey property collecting heartsease to complement the cordate design. As her pansies grew fruitful, Lady Bennett selected seed from the best of the crop, giving names to her favorite offshoots. Soon the former wildflower was earning growing space on Britain's best estates. By 1841, when the Hammersmith Heartsease Society was founded, there were no fewer

than four hundred named hybrids. The British were immensely serious about their pansies and featured them at fairs throughout the country. To win an award, a flower needed a handsome set of black "whiskers" etched in its face, and the petals had to be perfectly round. Only creamy white or eggshell blue varieties were permitted on show tables. Today we favor those monkey-faced flowers in all shades of the rainbow, the brighter the better. As cut flowers, pansies can be bunched closely in shallow vases or tucked, neatly overlapping, into ring-shaped holders sold especially for that purpose. But alas, any artistry will be short-lived: The flowers begin to curl a day or so after being cut. Intact plants linger a bit longer, and since pansies are usually plentiful, there is no harm in unearthing a stem with its little nest of foliage and flowers.

GEORGE ELIOT'S WORKS   GEORGE ELIOT'S WORKS   ARABIAN NIGHTS   THE RULING   NIGHT OVER WATER

longer and maintain their vibrant colors better when placed in a shady, cool corner illuminated only by incidental light.

But not all cut flowers are meant to last. In summer you can trim a rampant vine that has wandered a little too far and drape the clippings around a mirror, picture frame, or window casing. Any vine will do — clematis, passionflower, rambling rose, hops, honeysuckle, ivy. Slip the base in water, mist the foliage lightly, and hope for the best. The chain might last a day and perhaps linger into the evening as well. Over the next few days, replace your masterpiece with some fresh cuttings until the vine in the garden is pruned into bounds. Many annuals such as snapdragons, marigolds, and bachelor's buttons grow more bountiful if they are cut frequently.

In autumn, fill containers with every blossom that can be cut before frost puts an end to the lavishness. In the rush to rescue favorites, cast caution aside: Even slapdash bouquets have a charm all their own. Fortunately, autumn's flowers last much longer than any other cuttings, having been prechilled by the brisk air and prepared for life indoors by the season's shortening days. Those that withstand a light frost or two are all the more stalwart. Fall weather is perfect

Sturdy vines of hops, fully clad in conelike flowers, meander in a book alcove. Dried hydrangea adds the perfect accent. Pliable, nonwoody vines last nicely indoors, especially if the branch is anchored in an urn of water. ❧ ❧ ❧

In late summer, even a few maple leaves keep the season alive and add charm to a mantel arrangement (above). When the first frost threatens, lilies, cockscomb, love-lies-bleeding, foxglove, and ivy make a lovely eclectic grouping (opposite).

for conditioning flowers: There is no need to tuck them in the refrigerator before a special occasion; just leave newly cut stems sitting on the back porch or in a breezeway; they will have more strength than artificially prepared flowers.

Although autumn might seem a bittersweet time, tinged with memories of summer, it has many gifts all its own. As the chill deepens and branches turn fiery shades, bring maple leaves, sheaves of seed-bearing grasses, and berries clinging stubbornly to their twigs indoors. Such finds are just as handsome and colorful as open-faced flowers. Apples of every variety, pears, persimmons, pumpkins, gourds, and pomegranates are also part of nature's feast: Pile them amid the flowers, letting them spill over in sheer abundance.

If you planned your garden with a thought to the colder months, a few late-season bloomers will extend the harvest well past the peak of the season. Asters and goldenrod in the kitchen or chrysanthemums on the dining room table are delightful autumn traditions that are repeated every year; salvias, heleniums, sunflowers, sedums, dahlias, tansy, and yarrow perform until the

*I*n autumn, miniatures
such as potted dwarf
dahlias or marigolds in
glowing shades. should be
placed close to a window,
but at night they flourish in
lamplight. *H*ere they
share a tabletop with another
of summer's mementoes
— fern fronds pressed in
lacquer. ❧ ❧ ❧

first frost and make for some novel arrangements as well. Many flowers stage a second coming late in the year if they are picked right before they totally fade; salvias and snapdragons are two examples. Clipped and set in a vase, they will last well past Thanksgiving.

———— ❧ ————

If winter challenges your creativity, it also offers the greatest rewards. It may be the harshest season, but it is also the time we value flowers most dearly: Even the slightest sprig of greenery is treasured. Much of the season's finery must be brought indoors before the first snow. As the meadows begin to go brown, search the fields for intriguing seedpods and flower bracts to weave into wreaths and fashion into swags. Columbine, sedum, Siberian iris, love-in-a-mist, artemisia, and so many other perennials retain handsome pods long after they set seed. If you scavenge before brisk winds shear the garden bare, you can still find such wonders as dried hydrangea blossoms and the silks from clematis flowers. In winter, the garden's subtleties gain significance. In the herb garden especially, some verdant flora always linger, waiting to be cut and carried indoors. So many herbs remain green and vibrant even when stiffened by frost; horehound, santolina, and rue hold their color

throughout winter and keep their delicious scents frozen within. When you cut their stems and bring them indoors, set the tips in room-temperature water to thaw gradually. Later on, a warm room and a glowing fireplace will unleash the scents of each herb. For a stronger aromatic elixir, toss a few branches of rosemary, thyme, or bay leaves on top of the wood stove and let them slowly smolder, infusing the room with their heady essence. Cloves, cinnamon sticks, star anise, nutmeg, and other spices mixed with the herbs add a heady accent to the prevailing perfume; tied to swags and wreaths, they hint at the exotic.

With some silica and a little patience, the blush of roses, violets, lilacs, pansies,

Cinnamon sticks scent a grapevine basket dense with dried roses, hydrangea, cockscomb, and pinecones (opposite). A heart-shaped basket of miniature roses dried in silica is edged with bay leaves (below). ❧ ❧ ❧

delphiniums, and just about any other blossom can be preserved in perfect color and form. But even dried flowers fade in sunlight, so arrangements are best placed well away from bright windows. Keeping the blooms close together minimizes damage to the paper-thin petals and also gives the impression of fullness. Shimmering ribbons and bows add to the luster. Beneath the blossoms, deep in the bowl or pot, a little hidden potpourri adds a hint of aroma.

Midwinter parties at home deserve special floral arrangements, whether you choose sumptuous orchids, majestic calla lilies, or heavenly scented freesias for flowers. There is no need to show off rare flowers by the dozen; a few well-chosen stems in winter will catch more compliments

and turn more heads than the massive bouquets of more flower-filled months.

Houseplants slip into the limelight in winter, and forced bulbs seem magical, springing into flower just a few brief weeks from the moment their tubers are buried in soil. First, start paperwhites in forcing glasses for a rapid rescue from midwinter drabness. Meanwhile, cram shallow pots with lily of the valley pips and crocus, dwarf narcissus, and grape hyacinth bulbs. Forget them in a cold cellar or garage for a month or two, then put them in the windowsill when the first hint of growth appears. The most spectacular flowers, the fanciest bulbs, the most exquisite bouquets, and the dried blossoms of perfect hue should be reserved for your family's delight. That is the essence of the home.

Hydrangeas in a fruit bowl (right) and roses tucked into pine swags (far right) soften winter's starkness. Later in the season, flowering bulbs such as paperwhites are harbingers of the coming spring (opposite). ❧ ❧ ❧

Chapter Five

TENDER CARE: WORKING WITH FLOWERS

W̶ith proper care, flowers can be coaxed to last for several days in fine form. These sweet peas, roses, and lilacs were plunged into water the moment they were cut. ❧ ❧ ❧

T̶here is so much more to working with flowers than merely protecting and upholding the glory of a blossom. Floral design is the art of coaxing a branch to bend to your will. Working with flowers often means taking control of nature. At first, it might seem an impossible task to press a sweet pea to fall as you wish or to expect a rose to remain upright when it prefers to nod, but there are secrets that will allow you to accomplish those and so many other feats. When they are skillfully prepared, flowers can stay pristine in garlands for hours or stand firm without wilting in a corsage. With a little dexterity and cunning, you can persuade a flower to bestow all the beauty of the garden on your life and home.

So much of a flower's splendor is dependent on the care and treatment it receives from the moment it is cut. In florist fields throughout the world, harvesters rise at dawn to collect blossoms still heavy with dew. Flowers wilted the day before are revived by the coolness and moisture of night and full of stored strength, so sunrise is a perfect moment to gather them. Dusk and dreary or drizzly days are also excellent

times to cut flowers, provided they are not flagging from the ardors of the day.

Moisture is crucial to a newly cut flower. When the weather is extremely dry, give the garden a soaking throughout the night before you cut any blossoms; in fact, generous watering will coax a plant to continue producing flowers. Often, cutting gardens are thickly mulched with a bed of straw to retain moisture in hot, sunny regions and shaded in midsummer to filter the intensity of the sun's rays.

Flowers are best served if you bring a pair of clippers and a deep bucket of water when you go into the garden or field. For a clean cut, scissors or a sharp knife are more effective than pruners, which pinch the stem shut, blocking the intake of water. The newly cut branches should be plunged into the bucket and sheltered from the sun.

Most flowers should be captured when still in bud yet just beginning to show a hint of color. Cut open-faced daisies or carnations before the buds fully open. When selecting sprays composed of many flowers, choose a cluster with several buds still tight. Cut spires such as gladiolus and delphiniums when only a few lower florets are showing color; as the florets unfold, pinch off the spent flowers.

Flowers should be cut in early morning, while they are still dewy; scissors make the cleanest cut. Violets (above) originally had short stems, but were bred for length so they could be tucked and tied. Although petunias (opposite) have short stems, they should be cut as low as possible and the foliage trimmed away. ❧ ❧ ❧

*R*oses should be wrapped
in paper or foil, then plunged
deep into water to keep their
long stems from sagging. *The*
best florists give each stem its
own vial of water. ❧ ❧ ❧

Queen Anne's lace and lily of the valley form a mist of white in a shallow dish edged with variegated pittosporum (right). A single spray of cymbidium orchid is so intricate that it needs no extra adornment (opposite). ❧❧❧

While the bounty from your own backyard is just waiting to be cut and brought indoors, flowers in the wild should be collected only with the greatest caution to prevent sparse, shy, or endangered plants from being depleted. Unfortunately, at one time, before they realized the damage they were wreaking, overzealous florists were responsible for depleting many species. Even the handsome prince's pines, galax (wand plant), and Christmas ferns, once abundant in nature, have been put at risk.

If you come upon a modest stand of flowers in a meadow or forest, admire its beauty but leave it alone; take cuttings only when the blooms are profuse. Whenever you borrow from nature, leave some flowers and foliage on every plant to ensure that they will survive and set seed. Walk softly, disturb as little as possible, and become knowledgeable about endangered species. Rarities such as pitcher plants and wild orchids should never be collected; if you

(continued on page 113)

LILIES OF THE VALLEY

This tiny member of the lily family unfolds in profusion wherever there is a canopy of shade and a heavy misting of dew — by the banks of streams and in boggy thickets despite the harshest climate. Treasured throughout the world, the little bell flower has been known by a bevy of delightful common names — wood lillie, our lady's tears, lily constancy, mugget, ladder to heaven, tears of Holy May, and liriconfancie (a mouthful derived from lily convalle, alluding to the botanical name, *Convallaria*). By whatever name, the woodland flower breaks soil every May to send up gently folded

leaves, followed swiftly by a series of flower-lined spires. In ancient times, lily of the valley was associated with Ostara, the Norse goddess of the dawn. In medieval Britain, on Whitsunday, the seventh Sunday after Easter, townsfolk collected great armloads of the flowers to decorate their homes. In France, slender stalks of lily of the valley are still worn in buttonholes on May Day.

Many occasions are traditionally graced by this flower — christenings and communions, baptisms and birthdays, weddings and anniversaries. According to a Dutch tradition, a few lily of the valley pips should be planted in the newlyweds' garden; thereafter, the perennial blooming of the flowers is said to signify the couple's renewed devotion. The flower has also been credited with heightening romance: In ancient times, its delicate perfume was considered to be a love potion and its essential oil was deemed so valuable that it was hidden away in pure silver and gold vessels.

Although lily of the valley lasts a week or more in a vase, the flowers stay longer still if the pips are dug in autumn, potted in a mossy soil, and forced in a dark, chilly place for blooming in midwinter and early spring. When the first sprigs appear, bring them into a sunny window and watch the spires rise majestically upward. The sight is so lovely that some say the flower has the power to help all people envision a better world.

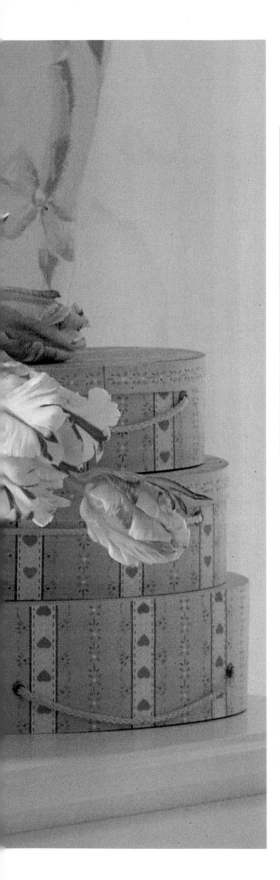

would like to use one in an arrangement, purchase the flower from a florist and request proof that it was propagated in a nursery rather than picked in the wild.

———— 🙰 ————

When buying flowers from a flower shop, choose blooms that are freshly unfolding rather than those half spent. If possible, make your selection from the flowers inside rather than from the sidewalk; sheltered flowers are not subjected to drying winds and scorching sun. Have the stems covered with a funnel of cellophane or plastic and the bouquet covered with wrapping paper to protect them from the elements, and handle them gently until they are safely home. Then submerge the stems in cool water and cut each tip, still underwater, at an angle. Mist any blossom that has begun to flag and gently pull off lower leaves that might steal moisture from the bud. Remove thorns from roses by clipping them off or rubbing them away with your thumb. Scrape the wood from thick branches of forcing twigs (such as apple blossoms and forsythias), evergreens, trees, and bushes so they can drink more easily. Then transfer the flowers to a vase where they can enjoy a conditioning period of rest and invigoration in

Unless they are wrapped in newspaper up to the neck while being conditioned, tulips will droop over in a vase. Sometimes, however, the graceful arch adds to the bouquet's beauty. These parrot tulips, displayed with their own foliage, are all the lovelier for the curve of their stems. 🙰 🙰 🙰

A teapot with its cover removed lends itself to a mixed bouquet of sweet peas, roses, and snapdragons softened by a frill of Queen Anne's lace (below). Sumptuous red roses find an elegant home in a crystal water pitcher (opposite). ❧❧❧❧

deep room-temperature water for at least two or three hours in a cool, dark place. Florists now have special refrigerators for the purpose, but estate gardeners used to simply leave their blossoms in unheated, moist cellars before arranging them in vases. While conditioning flowers, weak, floppy stems can be strengthened by wrapping them tightly in dry newspaper bound with a rubber band up to the bud's chin. This works wonderfully, especially for tulips and long-stemmed flowers such as anemones and delphiniums. Be certain not to let wet newspaper touch petals or leaves that will eventually be part of your display.

The next step is to prepare each stem for life in a vase. Crush thick stems of woody plants with a few quick whacks from a hammer. If stems are wide, make an inch-long slit up the center to encourage drinking. Euphorbias, ferns, milkweeds, and poppies will last for weeks if the base of the stem is quickly singed over a candle flame. The blush and vigor of hydrangeas, hellebores, anemones, and dahlias will last much longer if the lower inch of the stem is dipped for only a few seconds in boiling water. When subjecting the stem to these rigors, take care to wrap and protect the delicate flowers from the steam and flame.

Half the challenge and art of flower arranging is finding just the right container. The possibilities seem infinite, varying according to your mood, the surroundings, and the flowers on display. In a setting that is relaxed and intimate, watering cans, jugs, old canning jars, and crockery will do the job nicely. Certainly, containers that hold water are the most practical choices, but almost anything can be lined with a waterproof caddy and pressed into service. Baskets, wickerware, and terra-cotta garden pots can be fitted with plastic or rubber containers from the kitchen, with a little moss tucked around the top to hide the rim completely.

*Wayside weeds
such as bittersweet
and daylilies are fine
fillers for a bouquet
of daisies and Queen
Anne's lace (above),
but pitcher plants
(opposite), which
are now endangered,
should be purchased
from a nursery and
never taken from the
wild.* ❧ ❧ ❧

When the mood is more formal, lavish glassware makes elegant holders. Crystal, ceramic, porcelain, and fine china pieces all add to the luster of a celebration. For a subdued or monochromatic bouquet, an elaborate container becomes a lovely counterpoint. But a less ostentatious base is called for with an arrangement combining flowers of many colors. Clear glass reveals and often magnifies the stems, enhancing the lines of a tall branch or two, or showcasing the weave of many intertwined stems. If the clear view discloses a confusion of different textures,

hide it behind pebbles, marbles, polished stones, or glass beads. The stones provide more than mere camouflage; they hold the stems steady just where you want them.

For more elaborate designs, or with a container that does not hold water, floral foam, or oasis, with its puttylike consistency and ability to soak and retain moisture, is the most common contrivance for providing a base. The foam is conveniently lightweight, so if the flowers are long-stemmed or heavy, the oasis can be taped to the container's bottom to steady the bouquet.

Soak the foam in water until it is saturated, then place it in a waterproof tray. Other simple devices for anchoring an arrangement, borrowed from the professional florist, include crumpled wire netting, a pinholder (a comblike piece with many sharp pins that grasp the stems and hold them firm), a frog (similar to a pinholder but with prongs spaced farther apart), crumpled newspaper, or a network of fine twigs.

If stems are not long enough for your arrangement, or when you want to coax a flower in a particular direction, bend an inch of thin florist's wire at the tip and hook it just above the juncture where the bloom meets its stem. Thread it around itself and wind it down the stem so that both the flower's face and the stem can be bent and turned. Green florist's tape bound around wire and stem will camouflage the wire. When a bouquet begins to reach truly magnificent proportions, several layers of hidden containers are often necessary to support the heft. Completely concealed in the foliage, tall sticks holding plastic cones, tubes, or empty pill bottles taped to their tips can be filled with water or moistened floral foam to suspend the flowers. When skillfully performed, such contrivances seamlessly add another dimension to a bouquet.

To prolong the life of an arrangement, add floral preservatives to room-temperature water. Packets are available at flower shops, or you can make your own by stirring half an aspirin tablet in a pint of room-temperature water, or a few drops of bleach with a teaspoon of sugar in room-temperature water.

———— ✌ ————

The look of an arrangement will reflect your mood, the occasion, and the flora at hand. Since the beauty of a bouquet composed of only one species lies in its simplicity, foliage and frills would be superfluous. However, in a more complex rhapsody of many blossoms, the groundwork can be laid with foliage; a few well-placed pieces of fernery or evergreens serve as a foil, creating an airy effect and providing a network to hold the stems firm. Then the spires that furnish height and breadth can be put into place. Finally, fill in the space between greenery and accents with the chorus of many blossoms. So the bouquet is built — flowers are added, little by little — and living art is created.

Some arrangements are meant to be on the move. When a bouquet is destined to spend the evening waltzing around, proper conditioning is crucial to prevent it from wilting. Place the flowers for a hand-held

These long woody forsythia sprigs were cut in late winter. To help them take up water, the stems were crushed with a small hammer. A few pale salmon roses ground this airy bouquet. ✌✌✌

bouquet or halo in water for at least six hours before they are fashioned into an arrangement. To coax them to remain firm and properly positioned, run a wire up the stem and hook it into the neck of each bloom. Both wire and stem should be soaked for as long as possible, then wrapped snugly in florist's tape. If sheltered from the sun and slipped into water at every opportunity, a spray of hand-held flowers can endure in pristine condition for an impressively long time. All flowers hold their colors most vividly and remain lovely the longest when placed away from sun and drying breezes. Keep bouquets far from heat, radiators, and air-conditioning units. Mist the flowers daily and remove all petals as soon as they pass their prime. Change the water every day, recut the stems, and remove any branches that are flagging. With proper care, most flowers will hold their blush for a week or more.

Pressed into the pages of a heavy book, a flower or a few sprays can last for generations. To protect the pages from damage and plant dyes, slip the flowers between waxed paper or heavy tissue before closing the book and weighing it down.

A pressed bouquet carries a poignant hint of past glories, but blossoms preserved

Flowers such as peonies (above) or dahlias (opposite) that are to be carried in the hand should first be soaked in a tall vase and kept in a cool cellar or refrigerator overnight, then bunched and tied just moments before they are needed. Florist's tape wrapped around the stems will further lengthen their life. ❧ ❧ ❧

121

A *flower can be
preserved in near-perfect
form if it is cut just
as it is unfolding and
sprinkled with silica
powder. Roses hold their
form nicely, but almost
any blossom can be
captured and held this
way. Small, flat flowers
are the easiest to handle;
denser ones might
require a longer drying
period.* ⚘ ⚘ ⚘

*R*ose of Sharon,
Queen Anne's lace,
and daylilies are
easy to preserve in
silica; plump roses
and peonies might
take a bit longer
(above). Bright roses,
hibiscus, and
zinnias are softened
by hydrangea
petals sprinkled
among the colors
(opposite). ❧ ❧ ❧

in silica powder seem just as rosy and radiant as the moment they were plucked. Collect flowers for preserving when they are at the height of their splendor. Or if you prefer to capture a promising bud and seal it in time, pick it when it is still tightly furled. Preheat the silica powder for an hour in a 250 degree Fahrenheit oven to remove its moisture. When it is cool, spread it over the bottom of a plastic sweater box. Sprinkle the petals or buds thinly on top and cover them with another blanket of silica. Close the lid firmly and let the powder work its magic for a week. The

flowers will not hold their blush forever — they might fade over several months even if kept away from blanching sun rays — but they can look ravishing for up to a year.

——— ❧ ———

*D*ried flowers can also be used to create a variety of crafts; one of the most delightful is fashioning them into whimsical topiary forms and shapes. To create a fanciful topiary tree, for example, insert one end of a sturdy stick into a heavy terra-cotta pot filled with moss and attach an orb of moss-filled wire netting to the opposite tip of the stick.

A bouquet can be as impromptu as a few flowers of Sedum 'Autumn Joy' and a sprig of phlox set in a simple glass by a bedside (above) or as exuberant as a pastel confection of poppies, roses, calla lilies, and lisianthus proudly displayed in a 1920s pink bisque vase (left). ❧❧❧

Tuck rosebuds or other dried flowers densely into the moss, gluing anything that might not hold steady. The colors may fade with time, but the everlasting bush will gain a lovely antiqued luster.

Potpourri is another lovely way to use dried flowers. To capture the fragrance of summer, to explore the aroma of a flower and combine it with kindred scents and perfumes, gather blossoms for drying and stir them gently together. Rose petals, violets, tuberoses, orange blossoms, mignonette, lily of the valley, jasmine, lavender, rosemary, and so many other fragrant flowers and sprigs can be collected when they are just beginning to bloom. Spread them in flat boxes or hang them from the rafters of a dry, shady attic. In a pinch, if the weather fails to cooperate, slip them into an oven set at 110 degrees Fahrenheit for about forty-five minutes. Wherever you place the flowers, shuffle them often to encourage the petals to dry completely. When thoroughly dry, add one tablespoon of fixative, such as calamus root, sliced orrisroot, or storax, to each quart of petals. Then mix the aromatic brew together gently, combining scents slowly to create the perfume you want. For a hint of spice, gradually sprinkle in cinnamon, mace, vanilla bean, nutmeg, or citrus peel. Store your potpourri in a closed apothecary jar for six weeks, stirring the mixture weekly to make sure the various aromas mingle. Then bring it out and let its essence fill your home and seep delicately into your soul.

Many field flowers and herbs can be tied and hung to dry indoors (right), then woven into fragrant wreaths (far right). Violet potpourri takes its place next to fresh white roses (opposite).

A GALLERY OF FLOWERS

*"I can enjoy flowers
quite happily without translating
them into Latin. I can
even pick them with success and
pleasure. What, frankly,
I can't do is arrange them."*

CORNELIA OTIS SKINNER

We at *Victoria* believe that flower arranging should never be anything but a pleasure. On the following pages are some of our favorite flowers, in a rainbow of shades, in bouquets simple and informal. Next time you search for a very special color, or when you need a blossom of a certain contour or personality, wander through these pages and let our flowers spark your imagination.

*"WHITE
AS
AN ANGEL"*

— WILLIAM BLAKE

Alstroemeria
Astilbe
Baby's Breath
Camellia
Columbine
Coneflower
Daffodil
Daisy
False Queen Anne's Lace
Freesia
Gooseneck Loosestrife
Honesty
Iris
Lily
Peony
Snapdragon
Spider Flower
Statice
Stock
Tuberose
Veronica
Viburnum
Yarrow

WHITES

NICOTIANA

ORCHID

CALLA LILY, TULIP

COSMOS

GARDEN PHLOX

RANUNCULUS

132

BLUES

*"BLUE
AND
COOL"*

— DENISE LEVERTOV

BOLTONIA

GRAPE HYACINTH, SWEET PEA

DELPHINIUM

LARKSPUR

CORNFLOWER, CANDYTUFT

HYDRANGEA

Agapanthus
Aster
Bachelor's Button
Balloon Flower
Bellflower
Blue Spirea
Buddleia
Columbine
Flossflower
Forget-Me-Not
Globe Thistle
Hyacinth
Larkspur
Love-In-A-Mist
Lupine
Monkshood
Pincushion Flower
Salvia
Squill
Stoke's Aster
Veronica

"THE VERY
PINK OF
PERFECTION"

— OLIVER GOLDSMITH

PINKS

CHAMPAGNE DAISY

DIANTHUS

CAMELLIA

MANDEVILLA

PEONY

TOADFLAX

Anemone
Bellflower
Bleeding Heart
China Aster
Chrysanthemum
Cockscomb
Cosmos
Dahlia
Deutzia
Flowering Quince
Globe Amaranth
Godetia
Hollyhock
Lily
Obedient Plant
Phlox
Red Valerian

PURPLES

LAVENDER

COLUMBINE

CUPID'S DART

PRIMROSE

ANEMONE

IRIS

"GLEAMING
IN
PURPLE"

— LORD BYRON

Bee Balm
Butterfly Bush
Clematis
China Aster
Dahlia
Foxglove
Heliotrope
Hosta
Hydrangea
Lilac
Lupine
Ornamental Onion
Purple Coneflower
Salvia
Sea Lavender
Statice
Spider Flower
Sweet Pea
Veronica
Violet

*"THE
YELLOW
FLUTTERINGS"*

— JOHN KEATS

African Daisy
China Aster
Columbine
Daylily
Dill
Forsythia
Foxtail Lily
Freesia
Fritillary
Gladiolus
Goldenrod
Iris
Lily
Marigold
Mexican Sunflower
Mullein
Pot Marigold
Ranunculus
Snapdragon
Statice
Strawflower
Sunflower
Tickseed
Yarrow
Zinnia

YELLOWS

ROSE

EVENING PRIMROSE

LANTANA

LADY'S MANTLE

DAISY

DAFFODIL

ORANGES AND REDS

"THE ORANGE BRIGHT"

— ANDREW MARVELL

DAHLIA

POPPY

RANUNCULUS

BLANKETFLOWER

SCARLET FLAX

LILY

African Daisy
Alstroemeria
Astilbe
Bee Balm
Butterfly Weed
Cardinal Flower
Chinese Lantern
Crocosmia
Geranium
Gladiolus
Love-Lies-Bleeding
Marigold
Nasturtium
Pot Marigold
Red-Hot Poker
Safflower
Salvia
Sedum

BOUQUETS

Anemones
Sunflowers
Hydrangea
Yarrow
Dusty Miller

Top:
Lilacs
Lilies
Roses

Bottom Left:
Larkspur
Roses
Tulips

Bottom Right:
Alstroemeria
Daylily
Aster
Statice

139

Index

Photography Credits

Page 1 Steve Gross

Page 5 Wendi Schneider

Page 7 (center) Peter Estersohn, (background) Toshi Otsuki

Page 11 William P. Steele

Page 8 (top) Toshi Otsuki, (middle) Katrina, (bottom) William P. Steele

Page 9 (top) William P. Steele, (middle) William P. Steele, (bottom) Michael Skott

Page 12 (clockwise from top left) Toshi Otsuki, Toshi Otsuki, Toshi Otsuki, Toshi Otsuki, Toshi Otsuki, William P. Steele, Toshi Otsuki, Toshi Otsuki, Toshi Otsuki, Starr Ockenga, Toshi Otsuki, Toshi Otsuki, Toshi Otsuki

Page 13 (center) Toshi Otsuki, (clockwise from top left) Toshi Otsuki, Michael Skott, Toshi Otsuki, William P. Steele, Toshi Otsuki, Toshi Otsuki, Toshi Otsuki, Toshi Otsuki, Toshi Otsuki, Toshi Otsuki, Toshi Otsuki, Michael Skott, Toshi Otsuki

Pages 15-17 Toshi Otsuki

Page 18 Luciana Pampalone

Page 19 Nana Watanabe

Page 20 William P. Steele

Page 21 Nana Watanabe

Page 22 Luciana Pampalone

Pages 23-26 Toshi Otsuki

Page 27 Tina Mucci

Pages 28-30 Toshi Otsuki

Page 31 Steve Cohen

Page 32 (top) Toshi Otsuki, (bottom) Tina Mucci

Page 33 Michael Skott

Page 35 Doug Foulke

Pages 36-37 Toshi Otsuki

Page 39 Katrina

Pages 40-41 Wendi Schneider

Page 42 Steve Cohen

Page 43 William P. Steele

Page 44 Starr Ockenga

Page 45 William P. Steele

Pages 46-47 Toshi Otsuki

Pages 48-49 Wendi Schneider

Pages 50-52 Toshi Otsuki

Page 54 Wendi Schneider

Page 55 Jeff McNamara

Page 56 Wendi Schneider

Page 57 Toshi Otsuki

Pages 58-59 William P. Steele

Page 60 (left) Starr Ockenga, (right) Michael Skott

Page 61 William P. Steele

Page 62 Bryan E. McCay

Page 63 Michael Skott

Page 65 William P. Steele

Page 66 Toshi Otsuki

Page 67 Luciana Pampalone

Page 68 Toshi Otsuki

Pages 69-72 Toshi Otsuki

Page 73 Wendi Schneider

Page 74 Toshi Otsuki

Page 75 Michael Skott

Pages 76-77 Toshi Otsuki

Page 78 (left) Toshi Otsuki, (right) Luciana Pampalone

Page 79 Luciana Pampalone

Page 80-81 William P. Steele

Pages 82-83 Toshi Otsuki

Page 84 William P. Steele

Page 85 Toshi Otsuki

Page 86 William P. Steele

Page 88 Bryan E. McCay

Page 89 William P. Steele

Pages 90-91 Toshi Otsuki

Page 92 Michael Jensen

Page 94 William P. Steele

Page 95 Wendi Schneider

Page 96 Toshi Otsuki

Page 98 Steve Gross

Page 99 William P. Steele

Page 100 (left) Michael Skott, (right) Hedrich Blessing

Page 101 Toshi Otsuki

Page 103 William P. Steele

Page 104 Elvin McDonald

Pages 105-106 Toshi Otsuki

Pages 108-110 William P. Steele

Page 111 Toshi Otsuki

Page 112 William P. Steele

Page 114 Keith Scott Morton

Page 115 Steve Cohen

Pages 116-117 Toshi Otsuki

Page 119 William P. Steele

Pages 120-121 Toshi Otsuki

Pages 122-123 William P. Steele

Pages 124-125 Toshi Otsuki

Page 126 William P. Steele

Page 127 Toshi Otsuki

Page 128 (left) Luciana Pampalone, (right) Michael Skott

Page 129 Toshi Otsuki

Page 130 Michael Skott

Page 132 (top left) Toshi Otsuki, (middle left) Wendi Schneider, (bottom left) Toshi Otsuki, (top right) C. Warwick, (middle right) Toshi Otsuki, (bottom right) William P. Steele

Page 133 (top left) Nana Watanabe, (middle left) Toshi Otsuki, (bottom left) Starr Ockenga, (top right) Toshi Otsuki, (middle right) Toshi Otsuki, (bottom right) Steve Gross

Page 134 (top left) Toshi Otsuki, (middle left) Toshi Otsuki, (bottom left) Starr Ockenga, (top right) Toshi Otsuki, (middle right) Toshi Otsuki, (bottom right) Toshi Otsuki

Page 135 (top left) William P. Steele, (middle left) Andrew Lawson, (bottom left) Toshi Otsuki, (top right) Toshi Otsuki, (middle right) Michael Skott, (bottom right) Toshi Otsuki

Page 136 (top left) Toshi Otsuki, (middle left) Toshi Otsuki, (bottom left) Starr Ockenga, (top right) John E. Kane, (middle right) Toshi Otsuki, (bottom right) Toshi Otsuki

Page 137 (top left) Andrew Lawson, (middle left) Tina Mucci, (bottom left) Toshi Otsuki, (top right) Toshi Otsuki, (middle right) Toshi Otsuki, (bottom right) Toshi Otsuki

Page 138 Toshi Otsuki

Page 139 (top) Toshi Otsuki, (bottom left) Wendi Schneider, (bottom right) Toshi Otsuki

Page 144 William P. Steele

Front Jacket Wendi Schneider

Back jacket (background) Michael Skott, (insets, clockwise from top left) Toshi Otsuki, Wendi Schneider, Toshi Otsuki, Toshi Otsuki

Case Toshi Otsuki

Endpapers Toshi Otsuki